MASTER *of Leaves*

MASTER
of Leaves

Murray Silverstein

SIXTEEN RIVERS PRESS

Thanks to the editors of the following publications, in which some of the poems in this book first appeared: *The Brooklyn Review*, *California Quarterly*, *Edison Literary Review*, *Forge*, *Green Hills Literary Lantern*, *Hunger Mountain*, *In Posse Review*, *Jewish Daily Forward*, *The Louisville Review*, *Pembroke Magazine*, *Poetry Flash*, *Meridian Anthology of Contemporary Poetry*, *The Montreal Review*, *Nimrod*, *Poecology*, *Poetry East*, *Rattle*, *RiverSedge*, *Runes*, *Spillway*, *Tule Review*, *West Marin Review*, *West Wind Review*.

"The Teaching," "In the Beginning," and "The Wheeled Blade" appeared in the anthology *Chapter & Verse: Poems of Jewish Identity* (Conflux Press, 2011). "Song of the Traveling Salesman" and "Adult Fiction" appeared as a Pocket Poem in a series by Mrs. Dalloway's Bookstore, Berkeley. "October Time" was selected by Red Berry Editions for their 2012 Valentine's Day broadside.

Published by Sixteen Rivers Press
P.O. Box 640663
San Francisco, CA 94164-0663
www.sixteenrivers.org

Library of Congress Control Number: 2013917618
ISBN: 978-1-939639-05-9
Cover and interior design: David Bullen
Cover photograph: Lee Grossman, www.leegrossman.net

For Leo and Joe, in their turn

CONTENTS

He would hum over his old rigadig tunes while flank and flank with the most exasperated monster. Long usage had, for this Stubb, converted the jaws of death into an easy chair.

HERMAN MELVILLE, *Moby-Dick*

MASTER
of Leaves

In Monet's *Branch of the Seine Near Giverny*,
      a cloud of light on the near-still river,
the rolling green banks, themselves half-real,
      half-shapes-on-water; the river itself
taking its unselfconscious time; Monet, taking his cut
      at the river — spread my ashes there,
in that light, that river, and while you're at it
      baptize me, too. Awake before dawn,
he puts on his boots, the brown felt hat, wool socks
      and sweater, and crossing the road
through a mist off the meadow, reaches
      his spot. When light arrives, he's ready.
In his floating studio, moored to the bank, fourteen
      half-finished canvases around him, fourteen dawns
slowly arriving on each — scatter me there,
      in those mornings, Monet at work,
in those rivers, moving from each to each, the damp rising
      through the soles of his shoes. The deep
wants to enter a man, ask him certain questions — here
      the palest purple, here a true black-green:
Is *every* morning the mind of God, or only certain ones?

THE CONSTANT

Pulling weeds, after rain — the body of a woman
is the body of a woman, but the speed of light,

why, in the famous equation, must it be squared,
it's already the speed of light? — early spring,

tossing my pile on the compost pile. We're hit
with a double whammy in this life: sex and other people,

but there's heat, that feral almost-chocolate smell,
and twigs of cedar — twiglets — tangled in your hair.

In the land of the speed of light squared, m must long
to equal e. Or so a borrowed body thinks, hat askew,

sun on neck, hummingbird at the fuchsia — suck away, pal.

This peach, for example. Past prime, headed toward mealy but for cereal fine. I've heard about it, life, the scanning for patterns, but here it actually is: *If at any time you wish —* yesterday's odd robo-call — *to skip this message and hear the answer to life's most important question, press eight.*

Silence, I agree, is God. But so is Voice — a rebel god (the ticking toaster's going to *ding*), and kids the natural pagans. Still, *why?* I would ask, and *what? Of* what? And illustrations, please. Once in a diner — I was a kid — my father said, *Burn it!* sending back his toast. Cup of coffee, maybe, and jealous are the meek, but who sends back his toast? He was in women's sportswear, sales (as was his pa), lugged his samples everywhere, no store so godforsaken there might not be, he's going to check, a buyer in back. Good, we're survivors, Silversteins, our samples, our spin; bad, because the market rules. It giveth, he said, and it taketh away. The *-eths* were there to soften the blow. You mean *darker?* says the waitress. *No,* he says, and quietly this time, *burn it.*

But even if silence isn't God, voices are. Rebel gods. And poets the natural pagans. Here it is (thank you for waiting), the just-sharp-enough paring knife: you slice the peach, *ding* goes the toast, and you lug the departed, little butter, little jam, into the day on a poem.

SONG OF THE TRAVELING SALESMAN

Before I could do I was done
      by the West.
Before I was cool I was cold.

Before I was from I was free
      in the West
but before I could sell I was sold.

Driven from the East, by the North bounded,
      South-hounded,
and before I could tell I was told.

ON THE LAWN

So I'm lying on the lawn, the Great Ma
over in the laundry room, apron pockets full
of clothespins, Kleenex, and flakes of skin.

"Quit rubbing," the Great Pa would say.
"Quit rubbing," we learned to say.
I put my eye down up against a blade of grass —

why, I wondered, did she rub
& not just quit it like the Great Pa said? —
each blade has a fold, each fold

a shadow, inside each shadow, a spindle
of gold: saw, and never told.
"You'll rub 'em," he'd say, "to the bone.

I'm calling Dr. Rosenbaum."
"I'll be in the laundry room," she'd said
to me. "Wait here." And so I did

and so I have. And can report: *here*
is a lawn made largely of *her*, grief
a blade made largely of light. "To the bone,"

I say to my blade, "to the bone."

MONDAY

Socked-in all day, until,
               finding the thinnest seam of blue,
the sun slips under and underlights the fog,

and what, what was gloom,
               the whole muddled bay
of us, goes opal, opalescent.

But only for a minute.
               As if an eyeless creature were to turn
out to be all eyes. Or one big watery eye

watching itself, its own slow burn,
and we, our watching, fuel the flame

IN THE BEGINNING

And Grandson Leo comes to mind, squealing
with joy in my arms last week when I slobbered
with joy on his tummy, then, back flexed — the colic! —
something so quickly so wrong, he struggles
to arch himself free, free of this the slobbering world.

If the body is in pain — and it is — before it learns
to speak, are vowels the remnants of howls,
each word a vanished lullaby? To soothe
the ache of all that creating? The body *is* at birth
a wreck, sore and sorry — *what shore is this?*

Here's Leo churning at nothing, being changed,
the promise of some eventual saying, hands
reaching out to miss, then clasp, then miss again —
What's me? What's not? The thoughts, Leo, a body
must tend! To which I add maker, maker of shits.

And maker of shits-not-even, as when
your little brow was ploughed with furrows
and, *Thought!* I said to your pa. *Naa*, said Jake, *gas*.
I should have guessed, digest, digest! I was a brain-
riddled body once, sucked the breast *what's-me?*

Gnawed the bone *what's-not?* (But doesn't
it long to *be* thought, gas?) And later when
I wrote the note, "What's a body need?" the poem
answered, *Rhythm*, as in *And on the seventh day
He rested* . . . full of himself — all that creation —

and hungered for his not-self. In the dream
                              of a shattered form,
within the shattering, the form.
                  What shore is this, soul-maker?
                  And the poem answered: *Leo!*

CATHEDRAL LAKES, YOSEMITE

We jumped into Upper that morning, with a yelp
that changed the mountain. Just as our laughter
the night before seemed to change the lake,
the lake and her brother, reflected, the bottomless
moonless sky. *Ripple in still water*, sang the Dead,
and the cosmic thermostat flicked its starry furnace *ON*.

For us, one wants to think, sitting in the meadow
next to Lower next day, the sheer, ragged face
of the mountain impossibly strange. "The body
of the cathedral is nearly square," writes Muir, "the roof slopes
wonderfully regular . . ." and it's more within our compass,

but first comes the yelp, cry of dumb beginnings,
not the jay but its shadow, sweeping across the stone.

THE MOWER'S SONG

As the Partner in Charge of Infrastructure, I mow.
The memo from Salvation reads,
"Set your blade height high enough
to let the isotoma spread. It's *not* a weed." I know.

Taking out the trash, I saw its tiny pale blue stars
drifting through the lawn last night. Salvation, Moonlight,
& Giver to Spring in December of Reasons to Hang Tough,

her office the garden proper, current project, *Blight,*
attitude toward, & action in the face of. I am the Director
of Being There on Time, and the sign on her desk

reads TAKE OFF YOUR WATCH. I pipe in the music—
the blues, the ballgame, the Coltrane, the Creeley—
while she, in garden duds, conducts
the resurrection of the grass.

THE TEACHING

1. His Garden

I bring him home, sit him down on the back porch, and point to the garden, saying, *Tell me what you see.* HIS GARDEN I write at the top of the page, thinking, *This is going to write itself.* But, *A street,* is what he says, *a narrow, cobbled street. And a horse pulling a wagon. Old guy, tattered coat, has got the reins. Two kids. Legs hanging out the back of the wagon.*

I look. One of the kids is me.

2. In Cahoots

I'm under the table and won't come out. My father is telling the rabbi, *He says he's a rooster and won't come out.*

It was true, I was a rooster.

So the rabbi gets down on all fours with me and, *Ssshh,* he whispers, *don't tell: me too. And don't forget, as you go around being what is called a self, we're roosters.*

3. The Moral Clarity of Compost

He'd start a story saying, *Never, as a rule, tell anybody anything. But this is too delicious, and delicious overrules.*

He was going to teach me how to die but ran out of life to do it in.

Schmuck, he said, *that's the teaching.*

LAUNDRY LINES

Not even noon—quarter 'til—and everything washed
is hung. The empty basket; the all-but-inaudible song
on her lips in praise of a Saturday
quarter-'til-noon emptiness; the dying drip of droplets
from the freshly hung; all stories past and to be.

The drop that clings—is it the last? No,
the vacant watcher learns, caught in the lilt of her tune,
always next-to-last. Like a song
that longs to sing itself, the wings of desire
unfold in the kid however it is they do.

All day in the sun, the red checkered apron,
the socks and sheets, the loss-at-the-center-
of-all-tunes tune. The flannel shirt:
more new—can this be?—for having been.

THE POISON, THE CURE

for June 16

It's Bloomsday, I'm at the bookstore and in the door sails Finch, the old ex-actor, who dazzled the town all those years ago with his one-man mad Prince Myshkin show and never was heard from since. Never, word was, the same after that, so bonkers did he go playing the ecstatic idiot, but here he was — Finch! — storming the mic and barking, no intro, straight at me,

"— *YOU*, Cochrane, what city sent for him?"

He was Dedalus teaching Dublin kids the Greeks, and I, it appeared, was Cochrane, the Nestor episode. I drifted off — how *would* a city send for you? — returned to find him Deasey, the crackpot headmaster, telling Dedalus (who once again was me — so few had come for Bloomsday, a Wednesday afternoon, I was, I guess, for Finch, the smiling, all-purpose *you*), "Ireland is the only country which never persecuted the Jews. And do you know why?" he snapped. "Why?" I whispered. "Because [pause] she never let them in!"

He had this way, to punctuate, of rounding-while-bulging his eyes, one side more than the other. I remembered it from the Myshkin days, and here it was again, droopy and yet contained: still the morbid hysteric but on the downhill side. Saved, I wondered, was he, by his acting chops, like consciousness itself, first the poison, then the cure?

Two beauties, in skimpy tops and cut-offs, strutted past the store, the door propped open so I could hear the tall one saying "... my father's in*sane*—" and as a garbage truck crept by, caught in the afternoon bumper-to-bumper, its backup beeper on (why?), it came to me (Finch now morphing into

Molly, tossing in her bed), we made a sacred center, "you" and Finch and me — "Me," that is, if "I" were me but apparently "I" was not, being Cochrane to his Dedalus and Dedalus to his Deasy — and who was "I" now that he was Molly, seducing me with a sleepy stare, the un-purposed "you" of darkness?

EVERY DAY, it dawned, IS BLOOMSDAY

on our little patch of bookstore floor,

EVERY MAN A BLOOM!

Every frayed and fraying strand resolved around the fractal *we* — Joyce/Finch, you/me — while another smiling Joycean nodded to me from across the room.

All of us taking the waters.

And if not exactly sane, Finch — ex*u*ding Molly from every pore — san*er*. It was, I later learned, his twelfth consecutive Bloomsday at the store! You have to love this world. And the soul that must be the remnant of once having been a child, languageless, caged up in Finch, released in Finch . . . who, back now to being the gentle depressive, was thanking us all for coming, thanks, and thank you, thanking the store.

If it were easy, it wouldn't be a hero's journey.

I spoke to him after, told him I'd seen his Myshkin. "Next year," he says, "we'll do Bloom at the beach, jerking off, watching Gertie — the Nausicaa!" "I'll be there," I said, feeling Gertie-like already, and grabbing for my book, my bag, went backing out the door, where coming the other way now were my girls, this time the short one saying, "but we get to go to*mor*row—" as yesterday swam into my mind, out in the garage cleaning my tools, some of them my father's. Smell of the oil-soaked rag. And feeling for my keys—the smell contains the boy, the boy the man, the man the woman, the woman the darkness—"More," I prayed, "again and more," while Finch, unfurled, shouting, "Seeya," went sailing himself out the door.

DEEP EDDY

The grandkid and I, given a summer afternoon
To while away, we're at the springs, Deep Eddy,
Oldest public pool in Texas if I have that right —
Austin all around it now — and floating in its shallows,
Inching, inching into its deep, *Row row row your boat*
We sing to contain delight, the deep that's pouring out

Of us. *Everyone's a winner!* shouts a pale-bellied man
In a Longhorns cap, to half a dozen kids whooping it up
In the deep end. And thinking, *Maybe so, maybe so,*
I enter, reenter the song, make of its witless lunacy
The maddening endless round, *Life is but a dream* —

But no, the bottom disappears and suddenly it's not.
It's deep and cold and clear — feeling for the bottom
Of a summer afternoon, at Deep Eddy, locked together
Splashing, locked together singing, our four legs pumping
In a two-dog-paddle, one arm in a stranglehold
Around my neck: both of us have lost it and are real.

MOTHER GOOSE

When you said something about *your* mother,
　　　　My mother, I thought, white-as-a-ghost!
We were walking around the marina,
　　　　mothers on our minds, a flock of geese
out over the bay, mothers and Oklahoma.

When my sister eloped, my mother sat down
　　　　in a chair she never sat in, and wouldn't speak
except to say, *Tell him, Harry. She's run away.*
　　　　With Jack, my father said, *to Oklahoma.*
But what is that to the geese? The geese,

determined and lazing both (if that can be)
　　　　steadfastly fly-floating across the sky,
the blue-gray sky, the ribbon of geese, shadowed
　　　　upon the blue-green bay — so that
gray as a ghost was my mother, ghostly *green* her chair.

The world is the color of memory. But what is the world
　　　　to the geese? Tell me, if you know. I say
we can never know, but we can ask; below and over
　　　　the great green sea, vertical and swift, the lyric mind
was made to ask. But what is that mind to the geese?

ALL ABOARD

for Josiah Gibbs Silverstein, b. January 19, 2010

It's raining, it's raining, the it train is coming,
      we're lucky in here, the warm air rising
to ripple the drapes, in here we're the pattern of meaning,
      meaning the mystery of you, hello, Joe, it's raining!

It stopped, stopped, no, wait, a drizzle, between a fog
      and a drizzle, and keeps, what is, on coming;
all aboard, Joe, in just what light there is,
      it keeps — what dark — on coming!

The it train. You'll see: We're on it and yet
      we watch it go by. *How's it going?* people say.
Good, you'll learn — and rain is its blessing, tonight
      this rain — *good,* you'll say, *it's goin' good.*

WEDNESDAY

Another magnificent fog
burns to reveal the day: a man is a child

serving time. And feeling's the force
that fuels the pain, the balm

for which is mud, mud from the banks
of a delta plain. Life's big idea,

the word, contains the sun,
the sun the river, the river the pain.

ART TATUM

The kid in the club washing dishes
        who came out from the back to listen to me
was Charlie Parker. "Man, if I could play," he said,
        "like Tatum's right hand." I said, "Be both."
First you're the day and then the man out in the day.

I was blind but I could feel my mother's player piano
        playing "Piece for Four Hands."
First the storm and then the boy out in the storm.
        When lightning strikes does lightning feel?

I thought Fats Waller was God.
        And when Fats heard the terror in my "Tiger Rag,"
"Jesus Christ!" he cried, and showed me how
        a demonic intro builds to an easy swing.

One night in Chicago I jammed with Mozart's angel
        (I knew her from Toledo) "On the Sunny Side
of the Street." She was the street and I the folks
        out on the street. When we were done,
as the club emptied out, *Art*, she said —
        she called me *Art* that night —
See, for extra light, how I embroider you with darkness?

SHE WALKS IN

She walks in and fills my field and, emptied,
I-am-that, as the Buddhists say,
indefinite with meaning and crazy with hope.

But everything is do-able, *possible* —
shop, cook, clean, screw — nothing
so terribly subtle, nothing itself spells doom.

Love is delusional, I've noticed,
like the shining of the moon, and makes
the case for living you've been debriefed to lose.

DOING THE DISHES

I is another.
RIMBAUD

"She takes him *out* to eat?" "Once a month. He *likes* to eat."
"Stan liked to eat." "And does, he's *Stanley*."
"But he's not Stan. Does Kate see other men?" "There's one . . ."
"Would you?" "If you're asking if *you* have permission, yes,
you have permission — just don't abandon me."

"But — if it were me — it wouldn't *be* me." "To me, you'd be."
"You wonder if they ever meet, Stanley and Stan."
"Stop it, Mo, he's still one man!" "A *m*inus-one man."
"Meaning would *I* pull the plug? No, I wouldn't pull the plug.

He flirts, for God's sake, he flirted —" "I saw . . . with you . . ."
"And the nurse." "One, I don't call that flirting —
he can't, you know, get hard —" "You don't know that —"
"and two, it wouldn't —" "It's all about pain." "— *be* me,
the me that thinks —" "Stop with your precious thinking 'me.'

And would that be your *you/me* or your *me/you*?"
"Huh?" "See what I mean? End of conversation: busted."

LUNCH WITH SAUL BELLOW

"So," I say, "Saul, how *is* love lavished, anyway?"
"Sideways," says Bellow, "preferring the sneak attack."

"And *why* is it lavished?" "Easy," says Saul, "to keep
hate company, slogging its way to the heart, the heart

by way of the noggin." "And love itself is spun
from *what?*" I ask. "Stars," says Bellow, "and suns

that light the forms of love are metaphors for meta-love."
"Whoa!" I say, "slow down." "Dante," says Bellow.

"Ahh, but love and brains are housed," I say,
"in sagging and flagging bodies." "Joke," says Bellow,

"knock-knock." "Who's there?" I bite. "Soul,"
says Saul. "Okay," I say, "Soul *who?*" "See," he says,

like I'm taking his class, "not *what*, not *where*, but *who*,
Soul *who* . . ." And the doves in the trees whisper, *hoo-hoo*-cooo.

"Listen," says Bellow, draining his glass, "build a house
of stories, tangled with other stories — Augie begat

the Rain King for *Humboldt's Gift*." I stare
at his empty glass — he's dead. "Despair is for dopes,"

he says, "sadness the marrow of the want bone."
Hoo-coo, chime the doves, the invisible doves, *hoo-hoo*-cooo.

HERE WENT THE EGRET

I dug a pond, bought some fish, and here came the egret
To snag the fish. There's me, I thought, the pond,
The egret, the fish, and tiptoed out to watch her hunt—
You cannot buy an egret—and sensing me, she turns,
Gives herself a flap, then two, and rising,
Her legs, barely the concept of legs, first dangle
Then tuck up into the tank, the flapping becoming
Her stroke, stroking the morning, erotics of air, as up
And over me she glides and is and then is gone—
Patch of white between the trees. Her majestic is
Becoming her even more majestic was.

Over the gasping me, the thwarted and plunked
Forever down me, who dug the pond, bought the fish,
Thought there was me, the egret, the fish, but no,
                              there is only the egret.

GOLDFISH, AWAKE!

He claps his hands at the edge of the pond,
You who were perfectly fine
on scum and bugs, attention: Man is here!

and flings out his flakes of Science Grub.

Stop all your circling, darlings,
and come. Man, who remembers, believes
and betrays, man, the creator of death, is here.

TUESDAY

One night it dawned on him (years ago, a Tuesday),
       the day had only seemed to pass,
that what seemed Tuesday night was really Tuesday day,
       and what seemed Wednesday morning,
Tuesday night, etcetera. He'd always thought it
       the day with the most beautiful name
and was happy to think it the longest as well—
       why should they all be the same?
When Tuesday midnight finally came, it was
       Thursday 4 P.M., and he went to sleep
fearing himself completely out of sync. Then woke
       to find he'd found his lowest gear:
the one week took weeks, the next, months,
       until—and he could feel it coming—
a Tuesday that would never end. The sun
       rose on it one winter, and several summers
later it's 8 A.M. *What are they*, he wrote,
       the minutes, but a l w a y s, *unfolding?*

MOON IN DOUBLE BIND

Shock of the full moon's O last night—
      we were turning the corner home—
its halo doubled: O language: O night:
      the rush of it and then its pulse.

So let the crickets crank it up a notch
      and screw the words: we like to watch.
In this fix and of it—O, my old O:
      fresh stars and an infinite tango.

IN SCARLET TOWN

Go to any window and look out.
        Except it's not a window,
it's *Head of a Young Girl* by Vermeer.
        It's "Scarlet Town, where I was born."
 It's the *Pequod* sailing from Nantucket,
        the notion of Moby-Dick on board.
It's late afternoon in my Eden of guilt
        and I'm listening to Beethoven's Mass,
the *Gloria* of that Mass. Betrayed,
        betrayal, escape and remorse — check,
check, check, and check — salvation
        by metaphor alone. Make yourself
a nest in the piney woods, in the tall,
        bending grass by the lake.
But it's not a nest, no, it's *Young Woman*
        at a Window with a Pitcher,
it's "Sad-Eyed Lady of the Lowlands,"
        the flopping grass her hair.
Mistakes were made and all is lost,
        but go to a window and look out:
Let me call your attention to her lips.

THE ORGANIZER'S CALL

I hear it from the shore, the organizer's call,
               and organize me, I call back.

Crossing the street against the light, I see it in the look
                  of the young and elegant gal,
       and organize us, I look back.

I feel it when I touch
     the newborn's newborn skin,
                the organizing touch,
     and beating beneath my only heart, the organizer's heart.

You find it in old harmonies, the fogeys at their morning sex,
     a freshness in us we cannot destroy,
                we perfume the blade
                    with our need.

And late in night's soup kitchen, there he is
     to ladle it out: O taste of that
                which does not taste of you.

SONG OF THE FIELD

The song of the field is the buzz of the mind
    of the man in the field.
To enter the mind, enter the field.

But the song in the mind is the hum of the woods
    at the edge of the field,
and to enter the edge, you must enter the woods.

But the song of the woods is the caw of the crow
    at the top of the pine
and to enter the woods, you must enter the crow.

WHAT IS MAN? *

1. Blah-blah *Walk*

Blah-blah *walk* & I am up & prancing, yes,
but it's not what you think. The word, it's true,
releases all the old wild smells, glorious piss
of the previous dog, but then there is the leash,
its choke-chain & its leash. & so I am, I have become,
so-so on *walk*, the prancing merely Pavlovian.
Blah-blah *walk* & blah-blah *ball*—language, you wonder:
how can something scentless be so all so nothing
at once? Once! Once reality fetched itself.
The true masters, they say, can recall.
Mine can only yank. Out there in the sniffery
I find the perfect rotting plum, but he is eager
to get home & afraid of every window when,
in my delirium, I stake out my squat & release.

But after, I am content, am that which delivers the blows,
                    still can divine in remnants, remains—
        lavendercoldmorningwetsquirrelouttorun—
& was not this Oakland paradise?

2. In Which I Reveal My Name

Names are like little factories, one night I realized,
producing daily answers for confusions that arise
from your having so much, too much, I'd say, consciousness.

Mine is a fated given & to it I must reply.
So: Saul. After one of his writers. Whose last I forget,
but it's my last name too. *Solly!* he calls, up cocks one ear

& I rise knowing no Solly am I.
But who, one wonders, *is*? Or maybe *Who*, who wonders, *is*.
Like in your famous "Who's on First?" where
the dog's real name is Who,

but Costello, the little dope, never gets it—ha! Yes, no
question marks about it: who chews on this is nourished
by such as he is able—he Who is—
to suck out the marrow, amen.

3. What Isn't, Is

What is leaves you breathless, nothing needs saying,
don't try. & as for what is *not*, to say as you do—& I
hear this all the time—we haven't, my kind, a clue—

O lucky them, they know not of the terrible nothing
we're going & SOON to be! You're obsessed. We do
know not. I saw it before you could yank: elixir of seeing

the raw at last: that squirrel?—maggots were eating
its eyes. You lord it because you cook your dead.
& may you. But to suffer is one of the joys, pal.

Thus spake Saul & you can take that for a walk.
Appetite, I wish you, good canines
                          & furiously salivating glands.

As if the holy were made so by such & such a word.

4. On the Rug at the *Ulysses* Group

They got quite a chuckle out of this: — *dogs at each other's
behind good evening, evening, how do you sniff, very well, thank
you, animals go by that.*

Well, I could say a few things but, on the hole,
your Joyce has got it right. What makes us go.
Your Blake's *eternal delight*. (There was a Blake group, too.)

I could be a Bloom. Love a bitch like Molly.
Muse on thus & so & lo it would all cohere. In Molly.
But memory is short — wasn't I just a Sweeney? Stuck
up in a tree? *Sweeney Astray*. (I thought, at first,
it was *Sweeney* THE *stray*. You can learn quite a bit
lying on a rug.) Songs for the valley, songs for the wood —
oh, I could be a Sweeney.

It's strange: one day you're scratching fleas, the next
chasing shorebirds on a fresh-lapping shore.
O, I can make 'em scurry, but they get to fly.

Mad Sweeney could fly.

But if my bark releases them — I who am myself released
& breathless on this froth of sand —
who is it finally gets to fly?

Sweeney was mad, but he got a few songs.

Joyce, though, gets the Golden Seuss. On the strength
of his *yes*. When they said it out loud, the Molly,
someone whispered, pointing at me
on the floor, eyes shut, legs churning, *Chasing a rabbit!*
(I've heard this before.) No. It was the Molly I was in.

In and paddling, paddling o'er.
When she & Poldy meet (must mention this to Osip):
two dogs are going at it *on the street!*

The bark is limited, I agree, provisional. A barbaric yawp
not even. But isn't it our limits that allow us to see,
on the days when we do, beyond our limits?

What your great wroughters hath wrought
is faithful beyond command —
how do you do that, man?

(I love it that Molly loves Poldy for his mind.)

(His blah-blah *mind!*)

5. Osip

I mentioned Osip. Another lit-dog, a pal, whose man
upon receiving a smart-guy award, off they go to Mexico,
this mutt from the Oakland pound, & suddenly he's king
of the roof in Zacatecas, looking down the narrow streets

where the half-wild packs, the *perros callejeros*
as they're called, hold forth — each its butcher, its market,
its café, mapped on daily forays with the man.
Who otherwise sat tapping. "What's writing?"

Osip wondered, "& why?" "Osip holds down
the fort," the man would say to visitors on the roof.
& he did patrol perimeters, it's true, trotting back & forth,
snarling through the rail. But as the *perros* never even

bothered to snarl back—what did they care for a roof,
a man?—his was a war internal, his fort, for better
or worse, Fort Man. He could hear them mornings
down below—some bitch was always pregnant—

"—but we've got bowls," he pointed out. To no one!
& watching dust motes ride the rays of Zacatecan sun,
the man tap-tapping a Joyce on his box, "What *is* man?"
thought Osip lying on the cool tile floor,
                                    "that I am mindful of him?"

(His first question. There is another nose, he thought,
and it's inside this one.) "Humans, that I pay them heed?"

6. The Bone

Final thought (and then a surprise): inflicting pain
on another releases some pain in you. Too bad
it's so, but it's so. The overflow of loving yourself

so much. "Go home & kick the dog," you say. Well,
some water slops over the bowl. & more—no magic—
that which receives shall deliver the blow: the wound

is the world escaping. "Stay!" you say. & the word, I see,
's your leash. To that which cannot be leashed. The burn
of its rushing through your hand is, *aha*, the bone.

7. To the Falls! (in Which I Try My Hand) [possibly a series?]

Long ride, longer walk
                    into the ever saltier air.
        Time to dawdle, time to stare
& puzzle the bumbling bee-o,
                    & puzzle the bumbling bee.

Then onto the lake & into the lake,
                    plashed & paddled the cock-cold lake,
a stick was a snake, alive-o, alive-o,
                    a stick was a snake, alive-o.

Who Am was I, Who Am in clover,
            anxious, but not as,
                        in equal measure sun, desire.

To the falls, the falls,
            scrambled down, rolled over
                    —you would—& over,
the slap-happy falls, the silver-draped falls!

                                        —Saul

SELF-PORTRAIT

Looking up from the paper to stare out the window
where my image is reflected like a vanished twin.

They've found it, the God particle, it had to exist,
the math's too ugly otherwise, but now there's proof:

smash together protons at the speed of light
and there, for one-trillionth of a second, it is,

like molasses, they say, and haloed in darkness:
that which endows creation with mass.

Like the tiny drop of white in the black pools
of eyes in the Rembrandt *Self-Portait* at the Frick.

And the glowing speck of silver
on the top of his cane; the furrows of light

spilling down his chest, the golden paint-splattered apron,
cinched by a shadowy cord and a loose crimson sash.

Enthroned and self-annointed, he's fathered himself,
but also — pink blotch on the cheek, the whole face

battered like an old newborn — he's his mother, too.
Split a proton and there's God inside. This is not news

to God. But now, and if you understand the numbers,
it's Him and us face-to-face. Our kind

has figured it out, and our kind has seen it.
No eye contact whatsoever, though, at the Frick.

Stand there all day, he looks right through you
from under the brim of the Master's hat,

half his face in shadow. He's face-to-face
with something, himself — if nothing else —

endowing creation with mass. Call it *Self-Portrait*:
you watching him watching that.

ADULT FICTION

There is a book called *The Child*.
Everyone has a copy,
But it's never been read. You mean

To find yours, sit down someday
And give it a look. The blurbs
Say it's terrific — you laugh, you cry.

A signed first edition.
But where did you put it?
Where did it go?

DEAR METAPHOR

Trying to find you, speak your language, *is*, I say,
                      not *like* but *is*, the word itself
one of your legions, stand-in for something I can't ever know.

A return voyage: you were my first confusion.
A river is not a river; to have is not to hold.

That I set out late to find you, in what little light was left,
is my regret, finding, outside time, nothing, not even outside.

Good, I thought, there is a project for the stars. Druids
and pagans, Hopkins and Robbie Burns—all hands on deck!

Meanwhile, Mother, I'm moored in your night.
                           Any port in your storm.
(Who loves, could, a deadly, unchangeable One?)

Can I fix you a drink, old nourisher? Do you still drink?
Have you heard the one about the professor of theology

whose specialty is you? He brings a bucket of earth to class
and writes the word *ENCHANTMENT* on the board.

The word, itself—I hear you whisper—*one of my legions,
stand-in for something you can't ever know.*

OLD GUY WHISTLING

Old guy whistling in the locker room, terrible whistler,
missing half the notes. But felt, hearty—
I can make out the tune as I walk out the door—
it's "Thanks for the Memory,"
Hope's old theme song—bumping into the beauty
I saw on the treadmill: slender *and* curvy, I noticed,
but why, oh why, the tattoos, so many? Both arms
and one, the one on her back—turning to say, *Sorry, I—*
a goddess vine climbing down her spine
and vanishing under her shorts—
but *I* don't exist: she is whispering to her pal.
Both of them laved in dolphin light,
cloud-sprung, untroubled, late-September afternoon,
the pal whooping with joy at the news. Engaged,
I bet, or pregnant. The whoops now tangled
with the old guy's whistle, echo of—*I do exist, I do!*
Last day of summer, not quite, a gladness
rising to greet me, earth to the wheel giving thanks.

AT THE MUSIC CAMP

One kid alone on the road
         plugged into his iPod
drumsticks drumming invisible drum.

Above him in the dying pine
         a jay bangs away on his washboard.
Silence at the music camp.

Like using a day to look for a night.
         Invisible sticks, invisible drum.
The one kid. The jay.

REHEARSAL

Romeo and Juliet, Act III, Scene i.

Hot to practice his fight scene,
he holds the one good broom
and offers you the broken mop.
"Pa," he says, "how 'bout *now?*"

You're *the furious Tybalt*, he explains,
and have already killed.
When he'll say, *Now, Tybalt,*
take the 'villain' back, he'll flip the mop

to you, you catch it, and,
Thou, wretched boy, you get to say.
When, brandishing the broom,
he says, *THIS shall determine that,*

you'll make a thrust or two,
but mostly you're to block
and parry his; take the blade, be slain,
lie there on the linoleum.

Ready? You may groan going down,
but only a bit. You're only Tybalt,
no hamming it up. You may clutch
your wound, okay, as you fall,

just don't forget, *THIS*
shall determine THAT.
Got it? Let's go. Again. And again.
A Tybalt for a night, the colander

will slide off your head, clunk across
the kitchen floor; the mop will slip
from your moist grip,
and as the mother-prompter shouts

Romeo, away, be gone!
lucky you, you get, though dead,
to hear *him* cry, *O, I am fortune's fool!*

DRAWING THE GREAT LAKES

When he saw me on the rug, the map book open
to MIDWESTERN STATES, the ink-blue splotches
like a splash across the page, *I swam right here,*

my father said, pointing to Erie—the smallest,
like a puddle the big ones had dripped—*and fished.*
Walleyes, muskies. The people next door had a horse.

If all were interconnected, as my mother insisted,
one vast inland sea, son of one who'd swum in one,
was *I* not Great by extension? I traced them on a sheet

of onion skin, and she was right, all did touch.
Huron, I wrote, in thick block letters, my *H* trailing fire,
which pleased the old man, also an H. The whole business,

I could see, lit him up. *How's that map doing?*
We met, you know, on Erie, your Ma and me, on a dock.
I was with Whitey, asked him, Who's that?

And on the spot where Whitey said, *Her? That's Dottie,*
Dot, she's shy, I put a big fat Jewish star, colored it red
and wrote in Whitey's word balloon, floating above

my inland sea, *Dot, meet Harry*, and just above
my stick-figured pa, *How 'bout a swim? Sure*, said Dottie,
I'd love a swim. And off they go, let them,

into the swell and give of Erie. Headed for — I drew
the lines — Michigan, Superior, it's all one sea.
They'll need a north arrow, more blue, some green,

and when the names have faded, some good
mnemonic tricks to go by. Ontario.
The one that begins and ends with an *O*.

AUSTIN NIGHTS

One-hundred-plus-degree days. The grandkids,
Knowing nothing but such days, are fine with it,
But for a West Coast kid, trying to keep up,
It's passing-out time: hydrate or die.

But nights, *nights!* — bathe him, saith the Lord,
In perfect darkness. Sit him on the porch,
Give him a beer. Why, let him ask, am I here?
The dark-tasting night, like a river, answering,

Why is anyone anywhere? Let the crickcts
Do the talking. And the freight train; the last cars,
The drunken chatter over on the boulevard,
And the kids asleep, in their sleep. Nothing more.

Learning late to listen. Everything soothed
By darkness; everything close to its lyric core.

> *I was there . . . in that heaven which receives more of His*
> *light. He who comes down from there can neither know*
> *nor tell what he has seen, for, drawing near to its desire,*
> *so deeply is our intellect immersed that memory cannot*
> *follow after.*
>
> DANTE, *Paradiso*

Over a dinner to celebrate her thirtieth, and under the heading Life's Little Mortifications, the younger tells this tale:

I'm in nursery school — so, what, four maybe four and a half? — &
the teacher is asking one of the kids about his new baby sister, & the
kid's saying he was there *at the new kid-sister's birth. The teacher*
says wow & asks if anyone else's been there, seen *a brother or sister*
get born. My hand shoots up, and yes, I'm nodding, I was there!
And I'm telling what I saw, how it was, when the teacher inter-
rupts: "— um, er, but Annie," she says, "isn't your brother older *than*
you?" & I look at her, annoyed at her for interrupting me, & say,
"So?"

Big laugh, but she goes on: *& the teacher — the bitch — she just*
can't not *call me out, & "Sweetie," she says, "that's not possible"*
& so on & suddenly it dawns on me, my god, she's right: TIME. I
couldn't have! & just how crazy stu-*pid I must seem.* (The laughter
stops, becomes the murmur of congregants, but secular — *oh,*
man — a sprinkling of sighs.) *Talk about shame. My hand, I*
remember, went up to my mouth, I was so ashamed — I wanted to
push the words back in. The voices quiet, the quiet becomes a
space: at the temple of our listening, we pilgrims had arrived.

Someone said, *Reality!* Someone said, *Present at the creation!* Someone was pissed at the teacher and someone said, *So? is right!* until the younger she herself began to laugh, her eyes — *I mean I was* so *sure* — tearing now with laughter — *so friggin' sure!* And one who'd tried that morning to wangle himself around in time, thought *shame ÷ laughter = what?* and felt a wave of light pass through the cloud of his unknowing.

REREADING OTHELLO

He's nearing the end of rereading Othello—
Can you pick up the cleaning tomorrow?—
and *Huh?* he says, looking up from his page.

He is nearing the end of rereading Othello
and can't make the Moor see otherwise.
Can you pick up the cleaning tomorrow?

Here is a wife. Getting ready for bed.
In only her tattered T-shirt,
The cleaning, tomorrow, okay?

Forty years this bed's been made,
unmade, made, the tattered shirt
is the curtain raised—*Don't forget!*

He is nearing the end of rereading Othello
and must make the Moor see otherwise.

THE WHEELED BLADE

And He drove out the human and set up the fiery ever-turning sword to guard the way to the tree of life.

GENESIS, 3:24

Gellman. Who slugged me once. (Our families lived on a bungalow court, and wrestling over half a Danish I'd lashed out, off balance, no science at all, and missed my punch, when up came the uppercut, square to my guilty—it *was* his, the Danish—chin. His family moved, we lost touch, and here we were, the night shift: day one, summer job—at Piece O' Pizza, the original, on Beverly near Fairfax, in L.A., a first-generation neon *HAD A PIECE LATELY?* sign blinking above the door.)

LAWRENCE, it said on his PIECE O' PIZZA badge. He was on the Junior Manager track, and showed me how to shovel out the pizza pies and slice them into pieces with the rolling flashing blade. Gellman, of the quick criss-crossing slashing moves, the controlled and moral beauty of his rage.

Larry! I said, pounding out the dough, *Remember Judy?*

Judy Sharfman. Also on the court. Her father ran the Hebrew School. Crazy Judy. She let us look. Nympho, we called her, though all we did *was* look. She'd open her legs on her back on the grass then snap them shut. Jaw-dropped, I watched in wonder—as had been told: she didn't have one. Open, shut, open, shut. *I've seen that*, said Larry and chopped the air, karate style, timed to pass between the flap-flopping legs. Judy never flinched, then snapped her knees in a scissors squeeze and smartly mashed the hand.

Remember Judy?

Hell, yes! Sharfman, she was fierce. He spun his dough up through the air. *She wrote my Bar Mitzvah speech.*

What?

I didn't know that. Though I'd been to his Bar Mitzvah, watched him stand and *say* the speech. Did she write mine? I'd thought her father had. Mr. Sharfman. His starched white collar, his mustache meticulously trimmed. A few months before the big day, he'd handed it over, all crisply typed. *Here,* he'd said, *practice!*

Strange.

Yep, said Larry, catching the dough, *Rabbi Judy, she did Epstein's, too,* twirled it on his fists, then sent it spinning again, *wordstream from the cuntspring.* And I laughed, but the words startled, seemed fearsome, mysterious, holy almost. He saw my face and

wordstream from the cuntspring,

he whispered again.

And all that summer it became our mantra: Torah within the Torah, as, kings of the night shift, we sloppered tomatoes from steaming pots, cradled the bubbling lakes of cheese, lifted our voices and sang to the jukebox R&B, Elvis and Fats and The Chords. But just as I was getting the mind and body hang of it, the spinning, the ovens, the whirling blade, *clank,* one Sunday night went the lock: lights out; Gellman's in his Chevy yellin', *Seeya!* Piece O' Pizza's shut, and it was time, September, time—that other wheeled blade—to go.

FALSTAFF

My liar, my drunk, my father, my thief—
      "Prince," he says, "I give you the moon,
the moon in my sack."—my mother, my grief—
      "You'll be the King of Darkness soon enough."

BREAKING:

*It has been learned that time has formed a rebel training camp in
the foothills of the Northern Sierra.*

My watershed.
And has plans, sources say,
to infiltrate my days. The insurgent minutes
may already be at hand.
It's been confirmed, time's in control
of all strategic crossings. May stop and roll you,
switch you back, recharging all the while
itself with itself.
By moonlight.
Over death, experts say, the lyric.
But over the lyric what must be learned:
a sweetness in being no being.
Brush up against it, they say, and you'll see.

Details as we learn them.

GOLDSTEIN

They arrived, the olive trees, by truck one day
in battered crates stamped ARIZONA,
headed, we heard, for Beverly Hills.

Over a hundred—we counted—
in the fenced and empty parking-lot-to-be
across the street. Big enough to dapple

an L.A. dawn, and cool—someone came daily
to water them down—a world
of what was, made of what wasn't and filled

with what never could be. In nothing
but shorts and Keds, we boosted each other
up into the crates and clambered from tree to tree.

Goldstein, the fatherless, brought his father's knife;
his father's father's stolen-from-the-Indians-
who-stole-it-from-Kit-Carson *Bowie* knife.

Strapped it on ceremoniously. *I'm sorry,*
said my father—who'd known the Goldstein pa—
that makes no sense. And shouldn't you be keeping

out of there? No, said my mother, *I've seen that knife
and it* could *be. But not the father's father part—*
he was from Bialystok. And all are gone, so all

were wrong. But all are here so all are right,
at play in the woods of my half-assed knowing,
layer of gray, layer of green, until the destined spot

is ready—no doubt some movie star estate—
and here come the trucks, the crane. But first
came Goldstein, triumphant, 1949. Skinny kid,

look at him, he shinnies up the highest tree,
the questionable knife between his teeth, shakes the blade
against the sky and cries the ur-iambic cry, *Ta-daa!*

NOTE ON WRITER'S BLOCK

I learn my head is living in a shabby stall
at the edge of my old school yard,
and after work I visit it to watch it think.

It's dark in there, but I can see
a more disabled thing: a headless
quadriplegic frame. The head wants out

but says that it's afraid
to leave my body and live alone.
"I might think myself into a frenzy alone

and just snuff out." The body, meanwhile,
would love to shout, "Head, are you with me?"
but it hasn't any mouth.

"I'll just be a second," said T. and ran into Petco to grab a bag of kibble. Parakeets chirped in the window, in pairs of yellow and green and blue.

"I'll just be a second or two."

BEFORE YOU BUY A BIRD READ THIS, said the sign, PARAKEETS LOVE TO TALK & CAN LIVE TWENTY YEARS — $12.99. Ma's was blue. "I'm a pretty baby," Chipper could say

and, "Chipper's a pretty boy," too.

She refused to clip his wings. Let him fly around the apartment, shit where he pleased his white goo, my fastidious Ma — I still don't get it. My chore to clean the cage, the cage —

I'll just be a second or two.

Still no T. with his kibble. Can a poem keep vamping on nothing? No, not nothing! Ma was nuts about that bird, cupped him in her hands, ironed with him on her shoulder. "I'll freshen his water," she liked to say.

"Gives me something to do."

Not nothing: at $12.99, adjusted, Chipper cost over a buck! Plus the cage. The cage I found him dead in — here comes T. with his kibble — home from my first day of junior high, Ma a fine wreck for a week, a week — all just a second or two

or two, all just a second or two.

ONE WHALE

If you run into Ahab as you sail your seven seas
and hope to chat it up, be warned: all he wants
to know is, *Hast seen the white whale?*
If so, say so; if not, pass. He does not want to hear
about the grandkids. *How's the new book going?*
he will not ask. You'd love to say, *Yes, I saw him!*
Just last week! and watch the eyes widen,
but truth is, no. *I'm reading the book, though!*
you could say, *and I've been to Marine World,*
seen the orcas fly through hoops! Did you see
the movie? Gregory Peck plays you! But no,
no interest, sorry, pal, he's gone. Spend your life
at Marine World, thou hast not seen the white whale.

But you are not you! You're Captain Boomer
of the *Samuel Enderby*! Sailing past the *Pequod*,
on a clear sunny day, Chapter 100, page 500 or so,
and, *Yes!*, you take off your jacket, hold up
your shoulder-stump to prove — the whale-bone arm,
wooden mallet for a hand — *you have seen the white whale!*
And Ahab quickly boards — by the same sea cradled!
the same sea broken! — as from the quarterdeck you rush
to meet him halfway, clacking, like long-lost brothers,
bone-arm to bone-leg. *Speak!* he cries, and you call
for the good rum and the boy with the tambourine.

He's welcome to the one arm, you say, *but no more!*
and introduce *Dr. Bunger, carpenter of the* Enderby
who's also, you explain, *its surgeon* — *Bunger, Ahab,*
Ahab, Bunger — but you can't raise a smile.
And never will, you suddenly see: what's doomed
to be tragedy for him is, has become (and why

is the mystery, it's all one whale) comedy for you.
I'd rather be killed by Bunger, you try again, rolling up
your sleeve to reveal the bungled work, *than kept alive
by any other man!* But he's all squall, *When?* is all
he wants to know, *which way heading and spare
the tambourines.* And so is lost.

                                    But so are you.
Mates of the deep, you could have been
each other's heartiest welcomer. Late into the night —
break out the toddies! — you'd talk, you'd sing,
banging your cups to the shanty song, *We were there,
O, we were there, and wounded we turned away.
No more, no more, no more white whale for me!*

LINES FOR THE GRANDKIDS

Trying to claim the new, not knowing
which side is up, as day by day it claims you—
you'll see, Leo, it's been decreed: Appetite!

All must develop, to live, a taste,
some taste for the good and the true.
You can spit it out later, the logic is liquid enough.

All of this is written in the Book of the Child.
A book, by the way, which cannot be read
(see "Adult Fiction, " page 51). You'll need a job,

Joe, but also some work. I'll put in a word
with the boss. Having spent myself
some days a grunt in the Bureau of Saying.

DANCE

The shadow
stretching down
            the street today
was mine. I waved
            to make it wave,
pumped my knee
            to make it dance,
the two of us a tango
            making time
as we are being
            wasted
by time, slow gavotte
            of vanishing,
dance within the dance.
            When to lead
and when
            to let be led?

VILLANELLE FOR ALL I KNOW

The thinking never stops; it's the knowing goes.
Crosswords, the calculus — there is no cure:
the sun will set on what one thinks one knows.

The fastest way from here to there . . . all those
"proven" bromides for the soul prove the lure
of thinking never ends, just the knowing goes.

The up side is *not* knowing can disclose
a way of being in itself secure.
So let it set, the sun, on what one knows.

Before it hits the sea, a river slows,
becomes a brackish delta, not so goddamn pure.
The thinking never stops, the knowing goes.

Two plus two is four — just check your toes.
And family, family's our rock upon the shore!
The sun will set on what one's sure one knows.

Into the mother *un-* all thinking flows.
Ask Hamlet, Poldy, or Jude the Obscure:
the thinking never stops, what's certain goes:
the sun sets on the bay of all one knows.

A QUESTION

When she was young and a beauty
he could not say, *My beauty*.
Now the years are gone, he can,

can gaze and say, *My beauty*
and puzzle the puzzle of age:
when was she more the beauty?

AT THE ZOO

Gazing at the empty lion cage. Habitat. And *not* empty—
he's in there somewhere. Come back at feeding time.

Like searching Beethoven's biography for clues
about the Ninth—it's in there somewhere, come back

at feeding time. *Tyger! Tyger! burning bright*, I blurt out
in the snack line, Leo, five, smacking his lips.

Who wouldn't kill to feast on hot, juicy rhyme?
One hundred thousand muscles (but nary a bone)

in Mr. Elephant's trunk. You coil it up to fight
and lead with your tusks. It's words vs. music

by the end of the Ninth, and the music wins. Loses
its innocence but wins. And after the cotton candy

come the late quartets. Feeding time. The jumpy,
jarring tempos finally . . . soothe? Good grief, must explain

to kids without sounding like a schmo how I lost
the tickets to the Whirling Teacups ride. The instruction

is right on the score: Pluck it joyfully, the sorrow string.
Hey, *look*, Joe—diversionary tactic—one, two, *three* giraffes!

AT THE BALLPARK

They bring out the old guys on Veterans' Night
who doff—is the baseball word—their caps,
one hand steady on the walker while you cheer

as, overweight and overwrought,
that *Idol* gal sings the national anthem,
the umpire cries *Play ball!* and brushes
                    home plate 'til it glows.

This is your game, your team, your boys,
for reasons you cannot fathom—
if, after the fourth, no man has reached,
you will not speak the secret word.

I love it because it's tar-drip slow.
Whole Kentucky Derbies can be run
in what it takes this kid, watch him,
between pitches; the rookie, anxious,
he goes to the bag, scuffs at the mound—
it's Us against Him, Mr. Thirty Dingers,
who straps, re-straps, digs himself in,
each fidget being sacred as the lights take hold,
and for a splendid second all is one.

Slow, slow, then, BANG, the big thing happens.
But usually it doesn't: a lazy fly to left.

I could fly out to left! scowl trotting back,
secretly happy I made contact.

My boys, my boys, I wear your colors,
and terribly I care—but what's his name,

again, the kid on first? Each with a story
and something to hide: there's a sweet core
of sadness in baseball, *no joy in Mudville*, still.

(Why, for example, when most of the seats are empty,
don't you move a little closer to the field?)

Sad, but also divine up here, top of the bleachers, alone,
or as close as you get to divine, extra innings, under
the stars, big fat memory-moon—which side you're on
you'll soon forget. Did you see *that*? you'll ask yourself.
No, what happened? you'll say. No matter, for now,
"Vengeance is mine," says Tolstoy at the start of *Anna K.*—
        the salty peanuts, the one-dollar beer—"I will repay."

SOMEBODY'S SONG

The neighbor teaches drums. *Wham-bam,*
beginners pound, *wham*
bam-bam.

I've listened for years: rhythm
is bodied, beginners
get good.

Here's Mom going by, babe in a sling-pack
and cooing; Ma cooing back.
Very nice

but gone in a flash, the music
of what is, swaddled in
what was:

we listen for years, beginners embodied,
becoming, from nothing,
somebody's song.

IT'S HIVED AWAY, THE HONEY,
IN GOD THE GREAT BLANK

Time to write, to listen: the soft *pad-pad*
of the laptop keys — little clods of dirt
raining down on my enemy's grave.

> *That which receives the blows*
> *is that which must be split.*

Time to loaf and consider: the self-dissolving self,
hero of its own undoing, it leaves you left,
master of that, and leaving and leaves.

> *But that which must be split*
> *is that which cannot be split.*

It's come, the invitation, slipped under your door
in the night, requesting — black tie —
the presence of your absence:

> *that which must and cannot be split*
> *is that which receives the blow.*

MASTER OF LEAVES

1. Back Porch, Twilight

Back porch, twilight, garden on its late-summer binge;
striders all over the pond. My mother called them Jesus bugs.

They don't, though, walk so much as land, dimple, and drift
on water, give it—you can almost hear—a sideways *thwack*

to launch a sideways hop. Or hump, they hump the water
and drift, sparks of manic desiring alternate with perfect ease.

You, too, are a body; sink down in the butterfly canvas chair
and watch: light left, twenty minutes most. Each ripple

cradles a wiggle of vanishing summer light. But first,
more mania: into the dying a gnat storm is rising, a-jitter

like a worried thought: oh, dear, oh dear, the day is ending
but ending inside—oh, wait, oh, wait—the endless day.

2. October Time

October sun, the last of it, low and cold sober,
is blasting the plum,

turning its jam-dark leaves
to pale-green moons—they bounce the light

(also pale but yellow-green)
through the window and onto the floor.

October time.
And like the shadows

the foreplay
gets longer and longer. Lucky

are they
who watch

it vanish, October light.
Wait for them, October time.

3. The Master of Leaves

I watch them come and summer and turn.
I watch them fall. I bring
a select few of them into the house,
and, because it pleases me, I watch them rot.

I am the master of leaves. I rake
them into piles and then I photograph
the piles; walk among the fallen
and crush them under my feet.

Great master, our alphabet's an agony
of spine, a crazed, ecstatic branching after light:
south's our central finding — south
and a lyric for blight, e.g., red.

But tell about the North: does darkness taste?
Who guards the cave?
Is everyone so angry? Are there any trees?
And why are your lovers so impatient for the night?

4. October Walk with the Interior Gal

She'd read an early draft called "October Light,"
and, *You're right,* she said, *it's not the light we see,*
but things illuminated. Except it's heat you want,

not light; to kindle (from candle) *warmth for a night.*
There's light and the endless craving of light
to see itself, its shadow: your dead of winter

is my summer afternoon. The plum, though, is a plum,
he said, by virtue of its light — *but light itself is made,*
she said, *of light-eviscerated plums; wait your turn,*

you'll turn to light. He got out his keys. *Ask yourself,*
she said, *is this the moment before it rains*
or last week's evaporation? Looking up, he saw

the dark-dusted clouds. *The storm or the morning*
after the storm? The old lock is fussy. To get the key
to catch, you have to fiddle it as you turn.

He fiddled it as he turned. The door
creaked open, heat poured out,
and turning, he could see it was now raining.

5. On Hearing That the Neighbor, on Her Deathbed,
    Told Her Husband: "See You on the Other Side"

A year ago, just, we'd fixed the falling-down
old fence between us; I'd see her on the other side
all the time, taking in the laundry, calling for the dog.
We did holidays, politics, kids, and weather.

I knew the church was big for her, but not,
until the funeral, how: it's the House of the Word—
I am so dumb—and once the word is sung, the choir sang,
on goes the light, and see you on the other side.

But outside, this side, caught in the branches
of an empty birch, November light, the fall, *a* fall
was taking its toll. Golden a moment, then blown, rainy,
taking until the turn, the turn the tolling tolls

when on goes the light, the choirs sing—so dumb
it's brilliant!—and see you on the other side.

6. The Leaves Falling and Then the Rain

The leaves falling and then the rain
leave leaf-shaped orange-brown stains.

Like us on the lawn that sophomore spring.
The lawn behind the music school.

Just out of jail and all over each other,
Bach pouring out the window,

the Gamba Sonatas, allegro, falling on us
who were also allegro and on the immaculate lawn.

Afterward we looked inside. Empty.
Except for the prof who was teaching it anyway.

To no one. For the glory, you said.
And the stain. The leaves falling, and then the rain.

7. December Light

for Barbara Winslow

Looking out the window from his early-morning chair,
               what is, December 1, is light

through the fog and slowly gaining on the neighbor's red-
       tipped maple —
               as if a cloud were an ember.

Inside the window, the same light gathers
in the hour-shaped glass centered on the sill, its bouquet
of red tulips and pale feathered grass — whose stems
               he can see are becoming translucent —
               the one light
               through all.

To each according to his need, he thinks; from each
according to the mystery that through all, too, the one dark.

A professor of November light, he will study the claim of
       December.
He's biased, though, in the war against time, and on the side of
       the losers.

Why is *what is* so formal, he asks, and why is *what is not* so shy?
And why won't it yield itself, grief, to form, and always to form?

Because, says sad beauty.
Because and goodbye.

8. Someone with a Broom

It's December 22 and we did not come to an end.
Let the oak reconcile with its shade
                    and sing ding-dong bell.

Even the neighbor's pit bull wears a Santa cap.
I will leave no shits,
                    he promises, ding-dong bell.

All night we listened to Coltrane, glimpse of the real
messiah mind — sax circles snare circles bass,
                    he prophesies, ding-dong bell.

Someone with a broom was here. Wait, it was me,
I swept this path! Quick swipes, the old straw broom —
                    let the sweeper who forgot himself
                                        sing ding dong bell.

9. Winter Song

January 1, and a woman walking down the street
                    is humming "Summertime."
The song is the wish, and the song is the silence
                    around her wish,
a silence as she walked she made, and as she walked
                    and made, we pass,
and I, the head-down busy man, have suddenly
                    no place to go, desiring
nothing but desire and to listen with a listening bone
                    I didn't know I had.
One of these mornings, the famous words embedded
                    in the passing hum,

you're gonna rise up singing. It's Eros, *hello!* on January one,
                              whose song is the silence
and whose silence is the wish: *Then you'll spread your wings*,
                              I answer-hum — a silence
as we passed we made — *and you'll take to the sky*.

10. The Window

January sun on bare branches. Cold,
harsh light, softened by the same sun shining
on what's left of a web, shimmering
                              outside the window
like tinsel hung in the air.

And then the perfect crow flies by.

Not a scene to torture with questions.
Say goodbye to Mr. Crow.
The sun will set at the edge of the sky.
So long, Mr. Sun.

And words, these tokens of joy the world offered once,
are beginning to disappear
into the things they've named,
becoming *the tears in things*

                    the *web*

                              across the window,

the *window*, the *sash*,

          that impossibly delicate *light* in the *air*.

11. February Sky

Here comes my ancient mariner, baggy rain parka, hood up.
All you can see, like a flag of surrender, the ropey white beard.
He used to confront me, saw I was hopeless and quit.
Won't even look as I pass. Nor will the couple
sprawled on the steps of the middle school.
She's on her phone, in his lap, as *baby-baby*,
he whisper-moans, arms locked around her,
pressing his hood—his hoodie's up too—against
her indifferent back—kama sutra, if there's one,
for blank depression. As it starts to rain. The glow
off the phone washing her face. No, she *does* look up—
we're bodies and we're minds—sees me pass—and light
streams through us, lifts us up, returns us to the February sky.

12. Under the Plum

Late March. Warm. End of a dry wet-season.
No such thing as silence, yesterday on my walk,
the fragrant breeze, so undeserved: everything budding early.

But a children's song! Sung by the living
to all that are gone, with verses, refrain—the silence
under the plum, blossoming, everything showered in light.

NOTES

"Cathedral Lakes, Yosemite" is for Rick Millikan and Craig Tepper.

The middle section of "The Teaching" draws on an old Hasidic tale.

Though I can no longer find the triggering line, "She Walks In" borrows from Paul Goodman's *Little Prayers and Finite Experience*.

When, in Section 4 of "What Is Man?" Saul says, "—wasn't I just a Sweeney?" he's thinking of Seamus Heaney's *Sweeney Astray*.

The Dante epigraph for "Present at the Creation" is from the Robert and Jean Hollander translation.

"Goldstein" is for Richard Silberg.

In "One Whale," the phrase "heartiest welcomer" comes from William Butler Yeats, "In Memory of Major Robert Gregory."

"Villanelle for All I Know" is for my villanelle mentors, Lynne Knight and Carolyn Miller.

The sequence "Master of Leaves" is for Marsh, *To love that well* . . . The seventh section, "December Light," is in memory of Bella Dorin Llewellyn.

Thanks to Lee Grossman for the use of his photograph on the cover.

Finally, to the poet pals whose early readings and generous response helped shape this work—Helen Wickes, Richard Silberg, Carolyn Miller, Lynne Knight, Jerry Fleming, Ed Botts, Dan Bellm, Gillian Wegener—and to all at Sixteen Rivers Press, my deepest thanks.

Sixteen Rivers Press is a shared-work, nonprofit poetry
collective dedicated to providing an alternative publishing
avenue for San Francisco Bay Area poets. Founded in 1999
by seven writers, the press is named for the sixteen rivers
that flow into San Francisco Bay.

SAN JOAQUIN · FRESNO · CHOWCHILLA · MERCED

TUOLUMNE · STANISLAUS · CALAVERAS · BEAR

MOKELUMNE · COSUMNES · AMERICAN · YUBA

FEATHER · SACRAMENTO · NAPA · PETALUMA

Text type: MVB Verdigris Pro
Display type: Stempel Garamond
Printer: McNaughton & Gunn